A Measuring Rod to Test Text Books... in Schools..

A MEASURING ROD

To

TEST TEXT BOOKS, AND REFERENCE BOOKS

In

Schools, Colleges and Libraries

———

Prepared By
MILDRED LEWIS RUTHERFORD
ATHENS, GA.

———

At the Request of the
UNITED CONFEDERATE VETERANS

1919 ?

RESOLUTIONS BY UNITED CONFEDERATE VETERANS

The following Resolutions were offered by General C Irvine Walker of Charleston, S C, at the Reunion in Atlanta, October 8th, after Miss Rutherford's address on the importance of having the South's history correctly taught in our schools:

"Whereas, we have heard with the deepest interest the patriotic, historic, instructive and suggestive address of the illustrious Southern Historian, Miss Mildred Rutherford, Therefore Be it Resolved.

"1st   That our thanks are due and are hereby tendered to Miss Rutherford for her eloquent and truthful presentation of the facts of Confederate history.

"2nd   That we accept her suggestion as to having such facts imparted to the young of our country, so that they may learn correctly the rights and the history of that great struggle for which we offered our lives and gave everything save our sacred honor.

"3rd   That to make an organized effort to accomplish what she suggests, a committee of five be appointed, and if by it deemed practicable to carry out the same, under the authority of this federation

"4th   That the cooperation of the Sons of Confederate Veterans and United Daughters of the Confederacy be invited and each asked to appoint five members to form a part of our Committee "

COMMITTEE APPOINTED

At the Reunion held in Atlanta, October 7-11, 1919, the United Confederate Veterans resolved to inaugurate a movement to disseminate the truths of Confederate history

To carry out the same, the following Committee was appointed

GEN C IRVINE WALKER, Honorary Comdr.-in-Chief, U. C. V., Chairman, Charleston, S C

GEN. JULIAN S CARR, Comdr Army No Va, U C V., Durham, N C

GEN CALVIN B VANCE, Comdr Army Tenn, U C V., Batesville, Miss

GEN VIRGIL Y COOK, Comdr Trans Miss, U C. V, Batesville, Ark

GEN A J TWIGGS, Comdr. East Ga Brigade, U. C V., Augusta, Ga

The Sons of Confederate Veterans have appointed the following Committee to cooperate with the Veterans:

REV. J. CLEVELAND HALL, Chairman, Danville, Va.

DR. JNO. W. HOOPER, Roanoke, Ala.

W. C CHANDLER, Memphis, Tenn.

W. S LEMLEY, Temple, Texas

J. J. SLAUGHTER, Muskogee, Okla

A MEASURING ROD FOR TEXT-BOOKS

" '*A Measuring Rod For Text-Books,*' prepared by Miss Mildred L Rutherford, by which every text-book on history and literature in Southern schools should be tested by those desiring the truth, was submitted to the Committee. This outline was read and carefully considered.

"The Committee charged, as it is, with the dissemination of the truths of Confederate history, earnestly and fully and officially, approve all that is herein so truthfully written as to that eventful period.

"The Committee respectfully urges all authorities charged with the selection of text-books for colleges, schools and all scholastic institutions to measure all books offered for adoption by this *"Measuring Rod"* and adopt none which do not accord full justice to the South And all library authorities in the Southern States are requested to mark all books in their collections which do not come up to the same measure, on the title page thereof, *"Unjust to the South."*

"This Committee further asks all scholastic and library authorities, in all parts of the country, in justice and fairness to their fellow citizens of the South, to yield to the above request.

"C. IRVINE WALKER, Chairman "

* See "Truths of History," by Mildred Lewis Rutherford, Athens Ga, for additional testimony

A FOREWORD FROM MISS RUTHERFORD

Realizing that the text-books in history and literature which the children of the South are now studying, and even the ones from which many of their parents studied before them, are in many respects unjust to the South and her institutions, and that a far greater injustice and danger is threatening the South today from the late histories which are being published, guilty not only of misrepresentations but of gross omissions, refusing to give the South credit for what she has accomplished, as Historian of the U D. C , and one vitally interested in all that pertains to the South, I have prepared, as it were, a testing or measuring rod Committees appointed by Boards of Education or heads of private institutions and their teachers can apply this test when books are presented for adoption, so that none *who really desire the truth* need be hampered in their recommendation for acceptance or rejection of such books

Absolute fairness to the North and South is stressed as only *Truth is History*

MILDRED LEWIS RUTHERFORD.
Athens, Georgia

WARNING*†

Do not reject a text-book because it does not contain all that the South claims—a text-book cannot be a complete encyclopedia.

Do not reject a text book because it omits to mention your father, your grandfather, your personal friend, socially or politically—it would take volumes to contain all of the South's great men and their deeds

Do not reject a text-book because it may disagree with your estimate of the South's great men, and the leaders of the South's Army and Navy—the world can never agree with any one person's estimate in all things

But—reject a book that speaks of the Constitution other than a Compact between Sovereign States

Reject a text-book that does not give the principles for which the South fought in 1861, and does not clearly outline the interferences with the rights guaranteed to the South by the Constitution, and which caused secession.

Reject a book that calls the Confederate soldier a traitor or rebel, and the war a rebellion

Reject a book that says the South fought to hold her slaves.

Reject a book that speaks of the slaveholder of the South as cruel and unjust to his slaves

Reject a text-book that glorifies Abraham Lincoln and villifies Jefferson Davis, unless a truthful cause can be found for such glorification and villification before 1865

Reject a text-book that omits to tell of the South's heroes and their deeds when the North's heroes and their deeds are made prominent

Refuse to adopt any text-book, or endorse any set of books, upon the promise of changes being made to omit the objectionable features *

A list of books, condemned or commended by the Veterans, Sons of Veterans, and U D C., is being prepared by Miss Rutherford as a guide for Text-Book Committees and Librarians.

This list of course contains only the names of those books which have been submitted for examination Others will be added and published monthly in *"The Confederate Veteran,"* Nashville, Tennessee

---

* The endorsement of a series of Historical Novels "The Real Romance of History," was once given by the Historian-General, U. D C, upon the promise to change the objectionable statements regarding the War between the States The endorsement was used but the promise was not kept—her endorsement sold many books containing the falsehoods

† There was not time to submit this "Warning" to the Veterans or Sons of Veterans, but Miss Rutherford thinks it will meet with their approval

5

A Measuring Rod for Text Books

(See *"Truths of History,"* by Mildred Lewis Rutherford,
Athens, Ga., for additional testimony).

I.

THE CONSTITUTION OF THE UNITED STATES 1787, WAS A COMPACT BETWEEN SOVEREIGN STATES, AND WAS NOT PERPETUAL NOR NATIONAL.

AUTHORITY·

ELLIOTT'S DEBATES, Vol V., p 214.

"When the Constitution was outlined and read, the words *Perpetual Union* which had been in the *Articles of Confederation* were omitted Alexander Hamilton and others noticing it, and desiring a Union, opposed the adoption of the Constitution Some one moved to have it made a *National Government,* but this motion was unanimously defeated. Senator Ellsworth of Connecticut and Senator Gorham of Massachusetts have testified to this."

DANIEL WEBSTER, *"The Federalist,"* p 908:

"If the states were not left to leave the Union when their rights were interfered with, the government would have been National, but the Convention refused to baptize it by that name "

DANIEL WEBSTER, *Capon Springs Speech,* in 1851

"The Union is a Union of States founded upon Compact. How is it to be supposed that when different parties enter into a compact for certain purposes either can disregard one provision of it and expect others to observe the rest?

"If the Northern States wilfully and deliberately refuse to carry out their part of the Constitution, the South would be no longer bound to keep the compact

"A bargain broken on one side is broken on all sides "

DANIEL WEBSTER in 1833 said:

"If a contract, it rests on plighted faith, and the mode of redress would be to declare the whole void. States may secede if a League or Compact. '

HENRY CABOT LODGE says:

"The weak place in Webster's armour in the Hayne-Webster Debate was historical—the facts were against him. And Chief Justice Story in that controversy never once mentioned secession, he was only stressing nullification "

II.

Secession Was Not Rebellion

AUTHORITY:

DR. HENRY WADE ROGERS, Dean of the Law Department of Yale:

"When peace came it was found that the Articles of Confederation were weak, in that the Central government could not legally assume sovereign power—that power resided in those free, sovereign and independent States. and there was no delegation of any rights to a central head.

"It became necessary, therefore, to change the Articles of Confederation so that the States should be brought to coöperate, by realizing that the government should not be a *perpetual Union*, but an *agreement* by which certain rights were reserved for the Federal government, and certain rights were reserved for the State."

RAWLE'S *"View of the Constitution"* was a text-book used at West Point. Rawle said:

"It will depend upon the State itself whether it will continue a member of the Union."

"If the States are interfered with they may wholly withdraw from the Union " (pp. 289, 290).

"General Lee told Bishop Wilmer, of Louisiana, that if it had not been for the instruction received from Rawle's text-book at West Point he would not have left the United States Army and joined the Confederate Army at the breaking out of the War between the States."

BENJAMIN T. WADE, Senator from Ohio, 1858:

"Who is to be the final arbiter—the government or the States—why, to yield the right of the States to protect its own citizens would consolidate this government into a miserable despotism."

GOLDWIN SMITH of Cornell University:

"The Southern leaders ought not to have been treated as rebels—secession is not rebellion."

JUDGE BLACK, of Pennsylvania, said:

"John Quincy Adams, in 1839, and Abraham Lincoln, 1847, made elaborate arguments in favor of *the legal right of a State to Secede* "—*Black's Essays.*

AMERICAN CONFLICT, *Horace Greeley*, Vol. I, p. 359:

"Let the people be told why they wish to break up the *Confederation*, and let the act of secession be the echo of an unmistakable popular fiat. Then those who rush to carnage to try to defeat it would place themselves clearly in the wrong."

7

III.

The North Was Responsible for the War Between the States

AUTHORITY

THE NEW YORK HERALD, April 7, 1861

"Unless Mr. Lincoln's administration makes the first demonstration and attack, President Davis says there will be no bloodshed. With Mr. Lincoln's administration, therefore, rests the responsibility of precipitating a collision, and the fearful evils of protracted war."

THE NEW YORK HERALD, April 5, 1861

"We have no doubt Mr Lincoln wants the Cabinet at Montgomery to take the initiative by capturing two forts in its waters, for it would give him the opportunity of throwing the responsibility of commencing hostilities. But the country and posterity will hold him just as responsible as if he struck the first blow."

SHEPPARD'S "Life of Lincoln":

"Please present my compliments to General Scott and tell him *confidentially* to be prepared to hold or retake the forts as the case may require after my inauguration."— Abraham Lincoln

HORTON'S HISTORY, p 71·

"The withdrawal of the Southern States from the Union was in no sense a declaration of war upon the Federal government but the Federal government declared war on them, as history will show."

GIDEON WELLES

"There was not a man in the Cabinet that did not know that an attempt to reinforce Sumter would be the first blow of the war."

SEWARD said

"Even preparation to reinforce will precipitate war."

STEPHEN DOUGLAS said

"Lincoln is trying to plunge the country into a cruel war as the surest means of destroying the Union upon the plea of enforcing the laws and protecting public property."

ZACK CHANDLER wrote to Governor Blair

"The manufacturing States think a war will be awful, but without a little blood-letting the Union will not be worth a curse."

WILLIAM SEWARD said:

"The attempt to reinforce Sumter will provoke war. The very preparation of such an expedition will precipitate war. I would instruct Anderson to return from Sumter."

8

The War Between the States Was Not Fought to Hold the Slaves

AUTHORITY

A RESOLUTION was passed unanimously by Congress July 23, 1861:

"The war is waged by the Government of the United States, not in the spirit of conquest or subjugation, nor for the purpose of overthrowing or interfering with the rights or institutions of the states, but to defend and protect the Union"

ABRAHAM LINCOLN, in his Inaugural Address

"I have no purpose directly or indirectly to interfere with the institution of slavery in the States where it exists I believe I have no lawful right to do so, and I have no inclination to do so"

GEORGE LUNT's *"Origin of the Late War,"* p. 432

"A war simply for the abolition of slavery would not have enlisted a dozen regiments at the North"

Unanswerable arguments will be found in the facts that a slaveholder, General U S. Grant, was placed in command of the Union Army, and General Robert E. Lee who had freed his slaves put in command of the Confederate forces Two hundred thousand slaveholders only were in the Southern Army while three hundred and fifteen thousand slaveholders were in the Northern Army.

GENERAL GRANT (Democratic Speaker's Handbook, p 33), said:

"Should I become convinced that the object of the Government is to execute the wishes of the abolitionists, I pledge you my honor as a man and a soldier I would resign my commission and carry my sword to the other side"

SIMON CAMERON, Lincoln's Secretary of War, wrote to General Butler in New Orleans

"President Lincoln desires the right to hold slaves to be fully recognized. The war is prosecuted for the Union hence no question concerning slavery will arise"

Slaves Were Not Ill-Treated in the South The North Was Largely Responsible for Their Presence in the South.

AUTHORITY:

The servants were very happy in their life upon the old plantations WILLIAM MAKEPEACE THACKERAY, on a lecture tour in America, visited a Southern plantation In *"Roundabout Papers"* he gives this impression of the slaves

"How they sang! How they danced! How they laughed! How they shouted! How they bowed and scraped and complimented! So free, so happy! I saw them dressed on Sunday in their Sunday best—far better dressed than our English tenants of the working class are in their holiday attire To me, it is the dearest institution I have ever seen and these slaves seem far better off than any tenants I have seen under any other tenantry system "

MAJOR GENERAL QUITMAN of the United States Army thus described life on the "Old Plantation" in 1822 while stationed in Mississippi:

The mansions of the planters are thrown open to all comers and goers free of charge. The owner of this plantation is the widow of a Virginia gentleman of distinction, who was an officer in the last war with Great Britain

"Her slaves are a happy, careless, unreflecting, good natured race They are strongly attached to 'old massa,' and 'old missus'; but their devotion to 'young massa' and 'young missus' amounts to enthusiasm While in a way these slaves appear to be free, they are very obedient and polite and they do their work well.

"These 'niggers,' as you call them, are the happiest people I have ever seen. They are oily, sleek, bountifully fed, well clothed and well taken care of One hears them at all times whistling and singing cheerily at their work. . . . . .

"But a negro will sleep—sleep at his work, sleep on his carriage box, sleep standing up, sleep bare-headed in the sun, and sleep sitting on a high rail fence. Yet, compared with the ague-smitten and suffering settlers in Ohio, or the sickly, half-starved operatives in the factories and mines of the North and the Northeast, these Southern slaves are indeed to be envied They are treated with such great humanity and kindness "

CHAS E STOWE, the son of Harriet Beecher Stowe, in speaking at a negro college, said

"If you ask me if the slaves were better off under the institution of slavery than they are under freedom, I must in candor answer that some were—they were not fit for freedom "

Coercion Was Not Constitutional

AUTHORITY:

WILLIAM SEWARD to *London Times* Correspondent, Mr. Russell, April 4, 1861

"It would be contrary to the spirit of the American Government to use force to subjugate the South."

MR. SEWARD to Charles Francis Adams, Sr., Minister to England, April 10, 1861:

"Only a despotic and imperial government car coerce seceding States "

EDWARD EVERETT:

"To try to hold fifteen States to the Union is preposterous."

PRESIDENT JAMES BUCHANAN to Edwin M. Stanton, Secretary of War:

"There is no power under the Constitution to coerce a seceding State."

THE NEW YORK HERALD:

"The day before Fort Sumter was surrendered two-thirds of the newspapers in the North opposed coercion in any shape or form, and sympathized with the South. Three-fifths of the entire American people sympathized with the South. Over 200,000 voters opposed coercion and believed the South had a right to secede."

"*The Journal of Commerce* fought coercion until the United States mail refused to carry its papers in 1861."

CHARLES SUMNER said:

"Nothing can possibly be so horrible, so wicked or so foolish as a war against the South."

JAMES S. THAYER, of New York, on January 21, 1861, said:

"If the incoming Administration shall attempt to carry out a line of policy which has been foreshadowed, and construct a scaffold for coercion—another name for execution—we will reverse the order of the French Revolution and save the blood of the people by making those who would inaugurate a 'Reign of Terror' the first victim of a national guillotine." (Enthusiastic applause).

The Federal Government Was Responsible for the Andersonville Horrors

AUTHORITY

CHARLES A DANA, Assistant Secretary of War, said

"We think after the testimony given that the Confederate authorities and especially Mr Davis ought not to be held responsible for the terrible privations, suffering, and injuries which our men had to endure while kept in Confederate Military Prisons, the fact is unquestionable that while Confederates desired to exchange prisoners, to send our men home, and to get back their own men, General Grant steadily and strenuously resisted such an exchange "—*New York Sun*

GENERAL BUTLER said

"The reason for this was that the exchange of prisoners would strengthen Lee's army and greatly prolong the war "

GENERAL GRANT said

"Not to take any steps by which an able-bodied man should be exchanged until orders were received from him "

Secretary of War Edwin M. Stanton's statistics testify that while there were fifty thousand more of prisoners in Southern prisons than in Northern, the mortality among Southern men in Northern prisons was far greater

GENERAL GRANT, again, said

If we hold these men caught they are no more than dead men If we liberate them we will have to fight on until the whole South is exterminated "

This agrees with GENERAL LEE's *testimony* (*Official Records War of the Rebellion*)

"I offered General Grant to send into his lines all of the prisoners within my Department provided he would return man for man When I notified the Confederate authorities of my proposition, I was told if accepted they would gladly place at my disposal every man in our Southern prisons I also made this offer to the Committee of the United States Sanitary Commission—but my propositions were not accepted "

VIII

The Republican Party That Elected Abraham Lincoln Was Not Friendly to the South

AUTHORITY·

WENDELL PHILLIPS

"The Republican party is in no sense a National party; it is a party pledged to work for the downfall of Democracy, the downfall of the Union, and the destruction of the United States Constitution The religious creed of the party was hate of Democracy, hate of the Union, hate of the Constitution, and hate of the Southern people."

Again, he says:

"The Republican party is the first sectional party ever organized in this country. It does not know its own face and calls itself National, but it is not National, it is sectional. It is the party of the North pledged against the South It was organized with hatred of the Constitution.

"The Republican party that elected Abraham Lincoln is pledged to the downfall of the Union and the destruction of the United States Constitution.

"William Lloyd Garrison believed in the Constitutional right to hold slaves, and said the Union must be dissolved to free them.

"He believed in the Constitutional right of secession, so was willing to publicly burn the Constitution to destroy that right and called it 'a compact with death and a league with hell.'"

CHARLES BEECHER STOWE said:

"The party that elected Abraham Lincoln was a party avowedly hostile to the institution of slavery "

Had they not heard him say in his address at Cooper Institute that

"The anti-slavery sentiment had already caused more than a million votes which could only be seen by Southern States to mean a danger and menace Consequently when they drew the sword to defend the doctrine of States rights and the institution of slavery, they certainly had on their side the Constitution and the laws of the land, for the National Constitution justified the doctrine of State rights "

MR RAYMOND, in the *New York Times*, says:

"His election was more by shouts and applause which dominated the convention than from any direct labors of any of the delegates "—*Boston Courier,* May 26, 1860.

13

IX.

The South Desired Peace and Made Every Effort to Obtain It

AUTHORITY:

THE MISSISSIPPI CONVENTION sent a commissioner to Maryland and when asked what was the intention of the Southern States by secession, (Shaffner's "*Secession War*," London, 1862), he replied:

"Secession is not intended to break up the present government, but to perpetuate it Our plan is to withdraw from the Union in order to allow amendments to the Constitution to be made, guaranteeing our just rights. If the Northern States will not make these amendments—then we must secure them ourselves by a government of our own."

LORD CHARNWOOD'S "*Life of Lincoln*":

"This madness appeared when the Congress met in December, 1860 In order to allay the apprehensions of the Southern people regarding the purposes of the party just ready to come into power, the Southern members offered resolution after resolution looking to tranquility. These resolutions were all rejected by the House of Representatives.

"Then was offered in the Senate the celebrated 'Crittenden Compromise,' yielding all that the North demanded in regard to exclusion of slavery from the Territories, but insisting that the Constitution be respected as to fugitive slaves, and that the Constitution be maintained and its provision be kept as adjudicated by the Supreme Court of the land The South made no new request, it went not outside of the Constitution. It rested its case on the Constitution and on its interpretation by the highest court of the land. It was strictly loyal to the Constitution.

"Why was the Crittenden Compromise rejected? Because Mr Lincoln willed it He wrote letters to his party leaders to defeat it He said 'he had no compromises to make with the South.' The idea was that he had triumphed and that triumph meant no surrender in any respect of the new policies

"It was a tragic day when the Crittenden Compromise was defeated. Not a single Republican voted for it.

The Crittenden Resolutions were a most generous proposition from the South to allow out of the 1,200,000 square miles of territory acquired by conquest and purchase, 900,000 square miles for free territory and the remaining 300,000 square miles

14

to be free or slave as each new State formed might choose, and this, too, when Southern prowess had largely gained the territory. These resolutions in the interest of peace were offered by Northern and Southern Democrats Lincoln notified all Republican States through Senators Harlan and Zach Chandler to vote against these resolutions. Had he not done this they would have passed. Unjust as they were to the South, the South would have accepted them, and Thurlow Weed and Seward would have seen that they were passed by the North. It was Lincoln's fault they were rejected George Lunt said Lincoln later acknowledged that he regretted this.

Again Lord Charnwood said:

"Senator Chandler, of Michigan, had telegraphed to the Governor of Michigan to send delegates to the Peace Congress, 'but to send stiff-necked men or none—for without a little blood letting the Union will not be worth saving.'"

GEORGE LUNT, p 423, says:

"The propositions of the Peace Conference evidently formed a sound basis for settlement of the controversy. These resolutions were introduced by Mr Crittenden, of Kentucky, and had they been adopted, they would have saved the country from its coming trials On the committee of thirteen reporting these resolutions were Jefferson Davis, of Mississippi; Mr. Hunter, of Virginia, Robert Toombs, of Georgia, five from slave States—eight from free States. General Toombs reported to his constituents in Georgia that the Black Republican solidly voted against the resolutions Mr. Douglas, in the Senate, said· 'Every member from the South including *Messrs. Davis and Toombs,* from the Cotton States, expressed a willingness to accept the resolutions as a final settlement of the controversy Hence the responsibility of our disagreement, and the only difficulty in the way of an amicable adjustment is with the Republican party.'" (See *Congressional Globe,* Appendix 1800-61, p. 41).

"Mr. Toombs, in the Senate, said there were some conditions he would prefer, but for the sake of peace—permanent peace—he would accept them."

Mr Pugh, of Ohio, said he had heard the senator from Mississippi (afterwards President Davis) before leaving the Senate Chamber say he would accept it to maintain the Union. There is no doubt but that a two-thirds vote would have saved the Union "

When it came to a final vote *every Republican voted against them except Mr Seward who refused to vote at all* The resolutions were lost by a vote of 20 to 19 How could peace have been brought about?

Mr Dixon, of Connecticut, in 1860 had the true idea He said:

"The true way to restore harmony is by cheerfully and honestly assuring every section its Constitutional rights No section professes to ask more, no section ought to offer less"

Mr Brown, a personal friend and colleague of Jefferson Davis, of Mississippi, replied

"If that same spirit could prevail which actuates the senator from Connecticut, who has just taken his seat, a different state of things might be produced in twenty days"

The Rejection of the Crittenden Resolutions created a crisis

"The Southern leaders then called a conference What was to be done? All their proposals of compromise, looking to peace, tranquility, security within the Union, had failed They asked each other 'What is the purpose of this anti-South party? What means the rejection of our compromises? Why did Mr Lincoln discountenance any compromise? What means this secession from the Constitution? This refusal to abide by the decisions of the United States Supreme Court? What means Mr. Lincoln's attitude in opposing the Crittenden Compromise?'

"Despairing of their rights within the Union, the Southern leaders advised the Southern States to throw themselves back on their reserved rights and withdraw from the Union But it was too late It could have been done in 1850, but not in 1861 From 1850 to 1860 the North had educated the people of the North out of the Jefferson theory of State rights"—*George Lunt.*

Second Peace Congress, Ex-President John Tyler, President, Washington, D C

"Virginia did not act at the time with the Southern States that organized the Confederacy, but called a 'Peace Conference' Twenty-one States responded to the call The venerable John Tyler, ex-President of the United States was chosen president They met in Washington on February 4, 1861 But Salmon P Chase, to be the Secretary of the Treasury under the new administration, was there as the representative of Mr Lincoln and the new victorious party His speech destroyed all hope of any reconciliation He refused all compromises, and said Northern

16

States would never fulfill that part of the Constitution in regard to fugitive slaves, and that the decision of the Supreme Court would not be abided The failure of this conference was a great disappointment, especially to Virginia Mr. Lincoln took the same stand as he did regarding the Crittenden Compromise.''—Lord Charnwood's *"Life of Lincoln."*

JUDGE SALMON P. CHASE in Peace Congress·

"I must tell you further that under no inducements whatever will we consent to surrender a principle which we believe to be sound, and so important as that of restricting slavery within State limits "

And again he said·

"The people of the free States who believe that slavery is wrong cannot and will not aid in returning runaway slaves and the law becomes a dead letter "

Now, this was in defiance of the decision of the Supreme Court in the Dred Scott case

SECRETARY CHASE announced that·

"The Republican party would concede nothing in regard to slave extension in the Territories, and the Northern States would never fulfill their Constitutional obligations." (There was nothing to do but to adjourn)

THE third attempt was when the Peace Commissioners were sent from the Confederate government with this message:

"The undersigned are instructed to make to the Government of the United States overtures for the opening of negotiations, assuring the Government of the United States that the President, Congress, and people of the Confederate States earnestly desire *a peaceful solution of these great questions;* that it is neither their interest nor their wish to make any demand which is not founded in strictest justice, nor do any act to injure their late Confederates "

Vessels were manned and armed while the delegates were waiting in Washington, and were sent to provision and reinforce Sumter The last effort at peace was the HAMPTON ROADS CONFERENCE It failed (See Gen Julian Carr's pamphlet)

The Policy of the Northern Army Was to Destroy Property— That of the Southern Army to Protect It

AUTHORITY:

SHERIDAN'S OFFICIAL REPORT.

"I have burned two thousand barns filled with wheat and corn, all the mills in the whole country, destroyed all the factories of cloth, killed or driven off every animal, even the poultry that could contribute to human sustenance.

"Nothing should be left in the Shenandoah but eyes to lament the war."

SHERMAN'S *Memoirs:*

"It will not be necessary to sow salt on the site of Charleston after the Fifteenth Corps has done its work."

"One hundred million dollars of damage has been done to Georgia; $20,000,000 inured to our benefit, the remainder simply waste and destruction."

"On General Howell Cobb's plantation I told my men to spare nothing."

"I'll not restrain the army lest its vigor and energy be impaired" (p. 185).

"In South Carolina I kindled my fire with an old mantel clock, and a piece of a handsome old bedstead" (p. 225).

"Orders to kill Jeff Davis and his Cabinet on the spot" were found on the person of Dahlgren in Richmond, Va.

Lord Palmerson in the British House of Commons took occasion to express deepest indignation at General Butler's infamous order No 28 against the ladies of New Orleans

GENERAL GRANT to Hunter in the Shenandoah Valley, Virginia

"Nothing shall be left to invite the enemy to return."

' "City Point, July 14, 1864

" 'Major-General Halleck, Washington, D. C.

" 'If the enemy has left Maryland, as I suppose he has, he should have upon his heels veterans, militiamen, men on horseback, and everything that can be got to follow to eat out Virginia clear and clean as they go, so that the crows flying over it will have to carry their provender with them.

" (Signed)   U. S. GRANT,

" 'Lieutenant-General ' "

" 'City Point, August 26, 1864.

" 'Major-General Sheridan, Halltown, Va

" 'Do all the damage to railroads and crops you can. Carry off stock of all descriptions and negroes, so as to prevent further planting We want the Shenandoah Valley to remain a barren waste.

" ' (Signed)　　　　U. S. GRANT,

" 'Lieutenant-General.' "

" 'Headquarters Middle Military Division,

" 'Harrisburg, Sept. 28, 1864, 10·30 p. m.

" 'Brig.-Gen. W Merritt, Commanding First Cavalry Division:

" 'General: The general commanding directed that you leave a small force to watch Swift Run and Brown Gap and with balance of your command and Custer's Division to swing around through or near Piedmont, extending toward and as near Staunton as possible. Destroy all mills, all grain, and all forage you can and drive off or kill all stock and otherwise carry out instructions of Lieutenant-General Grant, an extract of which is sent you and which means 'leave a barren waste.'

" ' (Signed)　　　JAMES W. FORSYTH,

" 'Lieut.-Col and Chief of Staff to General Sheridan.' "

" 'Headquarters of the Army, Washington, D. C.,

" 'December 18, 1864.

" 'Major-General Sherman, Savannah:

" 'Should you capture Charleston, I hope that by some accident the place may be destroyed, and if a little salt should be sown upon the site, it may prevent the growth of future crops of nullification and secession.

" ' (Signed)　　　　W H HALLECK,

" 'Chief of Staff ' "

" 'Field Headquarters of the Military Division of

the Mississippi, Savannah, December 24. 1864.

" 'Major-General W. H. Halleck, Chief of Staff, Washington, D C.:

" 'I will bear in mind your hint as to Charleston, and I do not think 'salt' will be necessary. When I move, the Fifteenth Corps will be on the right of the right wing, and their postiion will bring them into Charleston first; and if you have watched the history of this corps, you will have remarked that it generally does its work pretty well

" 'The truth is, the whole army is burning with an insatiable desire to wreak vengeance upon South Carolina. I almost tremble at her fate, but feel that she deserves all

that seems in store for her We must make old and young,
rich and poor, feel the hard hand of war as well as their
organized armies

" '(Signed)   W T SHERMAN,
" 'Major-General.' "

Major Nichols, "*The Story of a Great March*, November 15,
1864 (p 38), Atlanta, Ga :

"A grand and awful spectacle is presented to the be-
holders of this beautiful city now in flames The Heaven
is one expanse of lurid fire The air is filled with flying,
burning cinders Buildings covering 200 acres are in ruins
or flames "

"We are leaving Atlanta Behind we leave a track of
smoke and flame Yesterday we saw in the distance a pillar
of smoke, the bridges were all in flames I heard a soldier
say, 'I believe Sherman has set the very river on fire ' His
comrades replied, 'If he has its all right ' The rebel inhab-
itants are in an agony. The soldiers are as hearty and jolly
as men can be." (p 37)

"The soldiers are hunting for concealed things and these
searches are one of the pleasant excitements of our march "
(p 39)

Sherman's *Memoirs,* Vol II, p 287

"In my official report of the conflagration of Columbia
I distinctly charged it to General Wade Hampton, and now
I confess I did it pointedly to shake the faith of his people
in him "

Gregg's *History,* p 375·

"The devastation of the Palatine hardly exceeded the
desolation and misery wrought by the Republican invasion
and conquest of the South No conquered nation of modern
days, not Poland under the heel of Nicholas, nor Spain or
Russia under that of Napoleon, suffered from such individ-
ual and collective ruin or saw before so frightful a pros-
pect as the States dragged by force in April, 1865 "

CONTRAST

President Davis:

"In regard to the enemy's crews and vessels you are to
proceed with the justice and humanity which characterize
our government and its citizens "

"General Lee, for fear his soldiers should pillage while
foraging in Pennsylvania, had the roll call three times
daily "

It is true General Early did burn Chambersburg, Pa , but it was only after a refusal by the people to pay the $100,000 demanded for General Hunter's destruction in the Shenandoah Valley

When at York, Pa., he was urged to burn that place in retaliation He said.

    "We do not make war on women and children."

GENERAL JOHN B. GORDON to the women in York, Pa

    "If the torch is applied to a single dwelling or an insult offered to a woman by a soldier in my command, point me the man and you shall have his life "

CHARLES FRANCIS ADAMS testified:

    "I doubt if a hostile foe ever advanced in an enemy's country or fell back from it in retreat leaving behind it less cause for hate and bitterness than did the Army of Northern Virginia "

R E. LEE, Commanding General, Chambersburg, Penn , June 21, 1863·

    "The commanding general considers that no greater disgrace could befall the army, and through it our whole people, than the perpetuation of the barbarous outrages upon the unarmed and defenseless and the wanton destruction of private property that have marked the course of the enemy in our own country

    "Such proceedings not only degrade the perpetrators and all conected with them, but are subversive of the discipline and efficiency of the army and destructive of the ends of our present movement. It must be remembered that we make war only upon armed men, and that we cannot take vengeance for the wrongs our people have suffered without lowering ourselves in the eyes of all whose abhorrence has been excited by the atrocities of our enemies and offending against Him to whom vengeance belongeth, without whose favor and support our efforts all prove in vain The commanding general, therefore, earnestly exhorts the troops to abstain, with most scrupulous care, from unnecessary or wanton injury to private property, and he enjoins upon all officers to arrest and bring to summary punishment all who shall in any way offend against the orders on this subject "

The South Has Never Had Her Rightful Place In Literature

AUTHORITY

HARRIET MARTINEAU said:

"For more than fifty years after the Revolution the best specimen of periodical literature that this country afforded was '*The Southern Review*,' published at Charleston, S. C., by Bledsoe"

HAMILTON W. MABIE placed Poe, Timrod and Lanier as equal in poetic quality with Bryant, Whittier and Longfellow. He said:

"In the widening literary activity the South has borne a very notable part—indeed, it may be said that it has borne the chief part."

PANCOAST, of Philadelphia, says:

"The Southern story writers have done more than given us studies of new localities We feel instinctively a different quality in their work Contrasted with the New England writers we feel the richer coloring, the warmer blood, and the quicker pulses When you read Hawthorne and then turn to '*Marse Chan*' and '*Meh Lady*' by Thomas Nelson Page, it is like passing from the world of thought to the world of action—from the analysis of life to true living. It is a world where the men are full of knightly deeds."

HAMILTON MABIE said:

"The genius of the Old South went into the management of public affairs and gave the country a group of statesmen that will not suffer by comparison with the foremost public men of any country."

Then again

"The South of today has no explanations to make; her quota of writers of original gift and genuine art is perhaps more important than that furnished by any other section of our country These writers exhibit certain qualities of the Southern temperament from which much may be expected in the literature of the future Their work comes from the heart rather than from analytical faculties It is made of flesh and blood, and it is therefore simple, tender, humorous and altogether human, and those qualities give assurance that it has long life before it."—*The Outlook.*

What does JOHN FISKE, a great historian of this century say?

While unjust to the South in many things he realizes the part the South has played in the making of the Nation:

"Jefferson, Washington, Madison, Marshall and Alexander Hamilton are distinguished above all others and in an especial sense they deserve to be called the founders of the American Union.

"The Declaration of Independence ranks with the Magna Charta and the Bill of Rights as one of the three greatest of State papers.

"John Marshall, Chief Justice for thirty years, settled the relations of the Executive, Legislative, and Judicial branches of the government

"James Madison, as a constructive thinker, did more than all others not only to create the Constitution, but to secure its ratification "

What section of the country ever produced greater orators than Henry Clay, John C Calhoun, John Forsyth, Benjamin H. Hill, Robert Toombs, Howell Cobb, Alexander Stephens, Robert Y Hayne, William H Yancey and a host of others?

The greatest American dramatist was Augustin Daly, North Carolina

In "*The Outlook*" in 1899 appeared this article from the pen of Hamilton Mabie:

"The South never lacked institutions to keep alive the best traditions of scholarship—never lacked culture to keep in touch with the best of thought and art in the Old World and the New A love of letters was really keener in the South than in New England, and there was a much larger group of highly educated men in the South than in New England—but ethics and religion made literature of secondary importance

"The genius of the Old South went into the management of public affairs, but it gave the country a group of statesmen who would add dignity to the most illustrious periods of statesmenship—such men as Washington, Jefferson, Madison, and Marshall—they will not suffer by comparison with the foremost public men of the country."

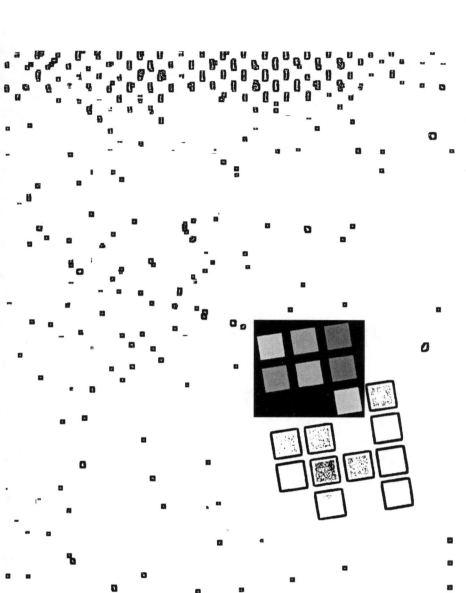

CPSIA information can be obtained
at www.ICGtesting.com
Printed in the USA
BVHW030939070722
641458BV00004B/318

9 781374 459670